Evoking Sound
The Choral Warm-Up

Choral Vocal Technique

Sabine Horstmann

Foreword and Introduction by James Jordan

Translation from German by Béatrice Mohar
Revision by Ingeborg Maria Mohar
Edited by Marilyn Shenenberger

GIA Publications, Inc.
Chicago

G-7424

GIA Publications, Inc.
7404 South Mason Avenue
Chicago, IL 60638
www.giamusic.com

From Sabine Horstmann, Chorische Stimmbildung (EM 1159)
© Verlag merseburger Berlin GmbH, Kassel
www.merseburger.de

English translation copyright © 2009 GIA Publications, Inc., under exclusive license.
All rights reserved.

Printed in the United States of America.

ISBN: 978-1-57999-737-3

This book is dedicated to the devoted singers who have worked with me through the years
and who have been willing to serve as the proving ground
for all of the exercises in this book.

My sincere thanks to Dr. Béatrice Mohar for the original translation from German, and
most of all I thank the lovely Marilyn Shenenberger for her never-ending patience and her
willingness to take on the project of completing the English edition.

Contents

Foreword v
Introduction by James Jordan vii
Introduction by Sabine Horstmann ix
Vowel Chart for Italian Vowels xi
The Vocal Instrument 1
Posture 4
Breathing 6
Sound 6
Exercises
    1–10   Relaxation and Posture 11
    11–17 Breathing 14
    18–36 Resonance and Relaxation 17
    37–52 Development of Sound, Equalization of Vowels
             and Register Exercises 23
    53–63 High Range 28
    64–69 Low Range 35
    70–76 Dynamics 37
    77–87 Diction 40
    88–94 Legato, Staccato, Martellato 44
Warm-Up Exercises with Movement for Children 47
General Remarks 51
Israeli Canon and Taizé Canon with Movement 53
Bibliography and Additional Resources 54
About the Authors 56

Foreword
James Jordan

It was July 1981 when I first met the great choral conductor Wilhelm Ehmann in a workshop at Westminster Choir College. As a result of a generous offer from Dr. Ehmann, this young conductor scraped together money for airfare to journey to St. Moritz, Switzerland, to study at the *Chorstudio Wilhelm Ehmann*. During those weeks, I sang and studied with figures who shaped a goodly portion of my musical and pedagogical life: Wilhelm Ehmann, Frauke Haasemann, Volker Hempfling, Welfard Lauber, and Sabine Horstmann.

I knew about Sabine before I arrived. Frauke Haasemann told me that Sabine was "her best student...ever." I remember thinking at the time: What a compliment! For those who knew Frauke, such compliments were few and far between. Frauke always held Sabine up as a model teacher and conductor. Frauke held the ability to teach others in a humane way as the highest of achievements. What I quickly discovered is that Sabine was the teacher's teacher. She is, simply, one of the best teachers I have ever met; that is, of course, if I don't consider Frauke Haasemann in that equation!

A Short History of *Choral Vocal Technique*

In America, the history of *Choral Vocal Technique* began with Frauke Haasemann's arrival on the Westminster campus in the fall of 1977 to prepare the Westminster Choir for a performance of the six Bach motets to be conducted by Wilhelm Ehmann. The rest, as they say, was history. Haasemann's pedagogy of building choral sound through the warm-up had profound effects on the choir college. This pedagogy, which she began and then built up to the time of her passing in 1991, is still in place today, continued by myself, Andrew Megill, and Joe Miller. Constantina Tsolainou was a close colleague of Frauke's during her years at Westminster and is one of the leading practitioners of *Choral Vocal Technique* in the United States. Also, her friends on the Westminster faculty, Irene Willis and Helen Kemp, strengthened the pedagogical foundations of teaching choirs to sing with the students who attended Westminster during those years.

After she arrived at Westminster, Haasemann co-authored her first book with Wilhelm Ehmann entitled *Vocal Technique for Choirs* (Hinshaw Music). As a result of that book, in 1985 Hinshaw felt that Frauke should be videotaped so her teaching would reach a wider audience. It was my privilege to lead that project. After that project was completed, Frauke wanted a book that detailed her pedagogy.

In 1991, *Group Vocal Technique* (Hinshaw) was published in addition to *The Vocalise Cards*. In the intervening years from 1991 to 2003, I discovered many other techniques to add to Frauke's already healthy legacy of exercises and text. In 2003, I published *The Choral Ensemble Warm-Up* (GIA). That book has three accompanying volumes of warm-up exercises, and now this book is Sabine Horstmann's pedagogical contribution to what was started by Frauke Haasemann.

Haasemann's strong belief was that the teaching of vocal technique to what she called "amateur" singers should be a joyful and humane experience, not an intimidating one. Perhaps no one understands this better than Sabine Horstmann.

Sabine Horstmann is one of the finest choral pedagogues I know. And like Frauke, though she is concerned with teaching vocal technique to those with little vocal training, at the same time she could teach a master class to the finest singers. More than anything, she understands how to make concepts crystal clear. Her exercises engage and challenge, and deliver sophisticated vocal technique in a humane way. Choirs love her exercises, but make no mistake: they quickly come to love her and respect her vast knowledge. Choirs love to sing for her and with her. My own experiences singing in choirs that Sabine has taught also shaped a great deal of my pedagogy.

This volume is more than a collection of simple exercises. It serves to further document the "next step" in the pedagogical legacy left to us by our beloved teacher and friend, Frauke Haasemann. These exercises also expand the materials already available to conductors as part of *The Choral Warm-Up* series.

Sabine is creative, humorous, fun, and a very astute teacher and conductor. She knows how to allow people to sing and to get them to sing with both honesty and beauty. This volume will quickly become one of our profession's most trusted and admired resources. There is no doubt that anyone who uses these exercises will be a better teacher/conductor.

I am proud to recommend these exercises to anyone who works with choirs and to introduce this gifted teacher to a wider American audience. While Sabine is my friend, she is one of my most valued teachers and mentors. This volume presents not only some of the magical ways she teaches vocal technique but also how she uses it to connect herself, in a very human way, to the singers she teaches. From my perspective, Sabine is simply one of the most gifted teachers I know.

Finally, on behalf of Sabine and myself, I would like to say that Frauke was not only our teacher, but our friend. She gave so willingly to not only us, but also to the countless thousands of conductors who came to study with her and attend her workshops on the Westminster campus. Suffice it to say there is not a day that goes by that Frauke is not with the both of us. The finest tribute any student can give to a teacher is to continue her legacy and ideas. And Sabine has done just that in this valuable resource.

—James Jordan

Introduction
James Jordan

In 1985, a very naive co-author (me) asked Frauke Haasemann if she had an order to what she did. Understand that was somewhat of a baited question, because I was very interested in detailing her method. When asked, she immediately replied, "Why, yes!" and within three days I had a typewritten note that she called "The List." The List, as it has become known, was the pedagogical ordering behind her ideas of choral vocal technique. That list has served as my guide and has not changed. And readers of this book will find that it is alive and well in Sabine Horstmann's work as well.

The List

- Relaxation
- Alignment and body awareness
- Relaxation of the vocal tract: relaxing the jaw, tongue, and lips
- Creating spaciousness (use of the sigh)
- Breathing
- Exhalation and inhalation
- Support
- Resonance
- General resonance
- Specific resonance
- Vowel development hierarchy
- Register consistency
- Dynamics
- Crescendo/decrescendo (*messa di voce*)
- Range extension upward
- Range extension downward
- Leaps
- Legato
- Staccato
- Martellato
- Diction teaching principles

This book is a stand-alone course in what the author calls *choral vocal technique*. Examine the table of contents and you will see that Sabine takes us through her own unique pedagogical tour of not only the "how" of teaching choirs to sing, but also the "why." This book can be used by conductors of choirs at all levels. In a very precise and compact style, Sabine's text contains a wealth of materials.

I am excited to bring this book to you as another part of the materials presented in the *Evoking Sound* series of pedagogical resources. It provides approximately 200 exercises to support the pedagogical process. Sabine's exercises are ones that I have used over the past twenty years, and they have never failed me. I hope you will find, as I have, a wealth of material to help you guide your choir to beautiful singing.

Introduction
Sabine Horstmann

Choral vocal technique is a most important element of working with a choir.

Everyone can sing! Singing is a natural expression of well-being and joy. Everyone has the capability to sing as well as to speak. Singers come to rehearsals because they enjoy singing.

However, they need guidance to be able to use their vocal instrument correctly. As with any other instrument, proper techniques are essential to produce the natural sound of the voice without un-natural efforts. Choral vocal technique can contribute to this in an important and fascinating way.

Inspired by the work of Frauke Haasemann, my teacher in the field of group vocal technique, I experience again and again with my own choirs how much the sound of the choir and its members improves when they are convinced of the importance of educating their voices.

Like swimming or playing tennis, singing cannot be learned from books. It would be helpful if all conductors had lessons in using their own voice properly so they would know how best to help their choir. Conductors are responsible for the singers´ voices. Therefore, they should know about the physiology of singing.

The vocal instrument is the only musical instrument that we carry with us *at all times* and that takes part in *everything* we do. It is, therefore, important to tune this instrument to its tasks at the beginning of every rehearsal and each time we sing. No musician in an orchestra would try to play an instrument while it is still lying in its case!

As in sports, muscular functions have to be trained regularly to bring about the best results with only minimal effort. For singers, this means they must have correct alignment to make efficient breathing possible.

It is the aim of choral vocal technique to put singers into a state of mental and physical relaxation, which allows natural singing without excessive exertion. A choir should never sound hoarse or strained at the end of a rehearsal. Singers should be made aware of their bodies as a musical instrument. They should learn to enjoy the ring of their voices and the sound of the choir.

There are two very different types of singers: those who use too much effort and are tense, and those who use too little energy and have too little physical tension. Both are using their instruments incorrectly. Usually inexperienced singers will use muscles that hinder the free flow of the sound (i.e., they may strain the neck muscles, protrude the lower jaw, or draw their tongue backwards). The most difficult task for singers is not to relapse repeatedly into these incorrect habits.

Movement is an important part of group vocal technique. Through movement it is possible to avoid many of the habitual errors in the use of the body during singing, and movement will help the process of adjusting the vocal instrument. Making music, and especially singing, refers to the development of a flowing sound. This is not a static process. This concept is exemplified in the original meaning of the word "choir," which signifies "a dancing and singing group."

Another characteristic of the vocal instrument is that in addition to alignment, the mental state of the singer has a great influence on the sound. It is well known that one cannot sing when tired or sad. Anger and stress change the sound of the speaking voice—and even moreso that of the singing voice! On the other hand, singing can free us from tensions and put us into a better mood. Many phenomena happen during singing of which we are often unaware and thus unable to analyze.

The complicated and delicate mechanisms of producing sounds are set in motion by the central nervous system. They are supported by the singers' *notion* of the sound. The hearing has an important control function. Good singing requires an attentive ear and an active imagination. The required sounds are brought forth by picturing and imagining. Thus, a conductor's imagination is especially critical during rehearsals to help singers place their voices properly by using evocative comparisons.

Choral vocal technique can:
- support a positive attitude toward singing
- take away the fear of high and difficult passages
- teach the basic techniques to meet the requirements of an individual piece of music
- form a homogenous sound out of many single voices

Choral vocal technique cannot:
- overcome all deficiencies of individual singers

Vowel Chart for Italian Vowels

VOWEL	IPA	EXPLANATION
i	[i]	Sing "ee" with rounded lips, showing rabbit's teeth (*not* with lips spread sideways in a smile)
e	[e]	Sing closed vowel with a lot of [i] in it
u	[u]	Sing "oo" with lips pursed and a lot of space inside the mouth
ü	[y]	Form an [i] vowel inside the mouth, surrounded by "oo" lips and a lot of space
o	[o]	Pure "o" vowel with a lot of "oo" in it
Open o	[ɔ]	Back lip vowel, as in the English word "often"
a	[ɑ]	Forward tongue vowel as in the English word "pasta"

The Vocal Instrument

The singing voice, as with all other instruments, possesses three qualities essential to creating sound:

- An element capable of vibrating: the vocal cords
- A force that causes vibration and keeps it going: the breathing
- Resonance chambers that amplify the vibrations and make them audible: mouth and trachea as the vocal tract, along with the cavities of the head and the thorax

These functions become clear when compared with an organ pipe:

Figure 1. Similarities between an organ pipe and the singing voice.

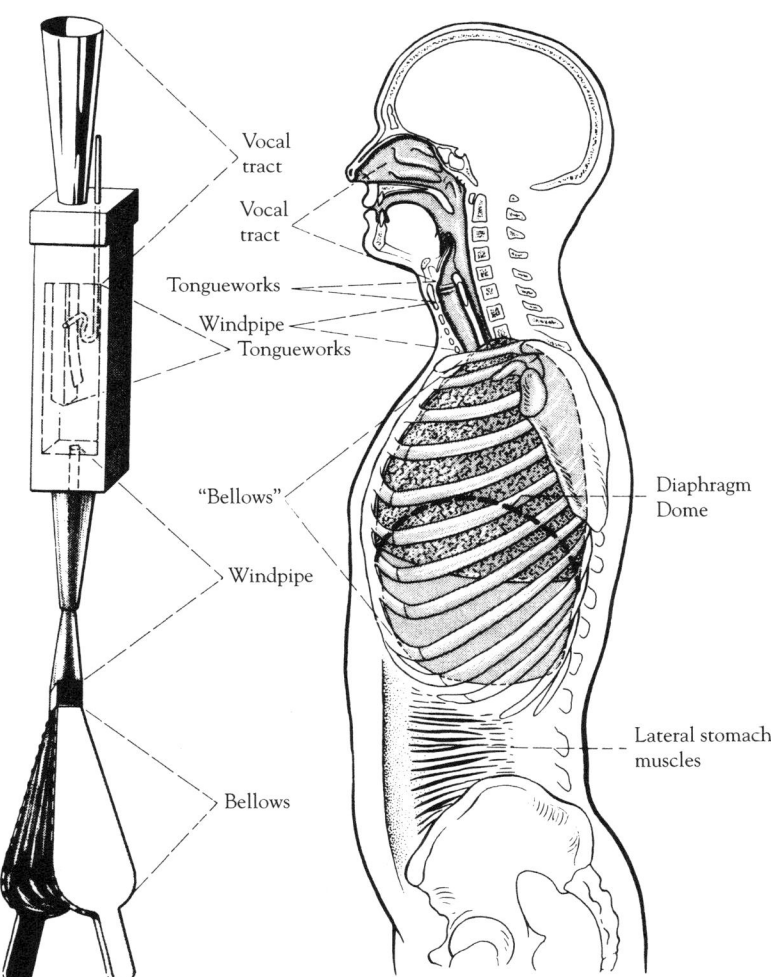

Figure 1: The construction of the human vocal instrument in comparison with the reed pipe of the organ (according to Barth) from: Günther Habermann "Stimme und Sprache" ("voice and speech"), Georg Thieme Verlag, Stuttgart 1978, drawing: Rudolf Brammer.

Vocal Cords

The vocal cords consist of muscle fibers that are able to contract and relax individually. The space between the vocal cords is called the *glottis*. The tension of the vocal cords alters the form of the glottis, which consequently alters the sound of the voice. The glottis opens during respiration and closes for the formation of sounds. The vocal cords are fixed in the larynx in a complex way. The larynx separates the trachea or windpipe from the oesophagus.

Respiratory Organs

The respiratory organs, similar to the bellows of an organ, provide the air and wind pressure necessary to maintain the vibration of the vocal cords. They consist of the lungs and the diaphragm as the principle respiratory muscle. The latter extends horizontally and separates the abdominal from the thoracic cavity. Breathing is controlled by the central nervous system (CNS), and it happens without conscious thought. The diaphragm is fixed anterior to the mobile ribs and posterior to the inside of the back.

It works like a pressure pump: In a state of oxygen deficiency, the diaphragm is given an impulse from the central nervous system, which causes it to contract and lower. This leads to low pressure in the lungs, which causes air to stream in.

During exhalation, the diaphragm rises and presses the air out of the lungs through the glottis. To enforce exhalation, the abdominal and intercostal muscles of the lower, mobile ribs come into action. Visible and palpable signs of diaphragmatic breathing are the rising and lowering of the abdominal wall. The diaphragm itself is not palpable.

Resonance Chamber

The most important resonance chamber is the vocal tract—the space between lips and vocal cords. It includes the lower, middle, and upper pharynx; the oral cavity; and the nasal cavities. This is the only resonance chamber over which we have influence. In addition, singers can feel the vibrations of their voice in the skull, the sinus cavities, and the breastbone. Sensing these vibrations helps to achieve good placement of the voice.

Posture

One of the prerequisites for singing is correct alignment, which alone guarantees adequate control of the breath and, thus, free development of the sound. Singers stand upright, spine erect, head well supported, neck and shoulders relaxed. The weight of the body rests evenly on both feet; the knees are not straightened but slightly flexed. The pelvis is kept straight.

Figure 2. Alignment of the spine and body shape.

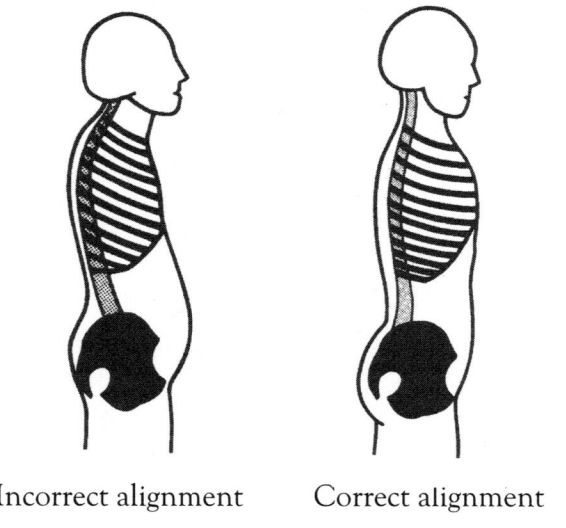

Incorrect alignment   Correct alignment

Figure 2: Dr. J. Parow: "Stimmschulung" ("Group vocal technique"). Paracelsus Verlag (Hippokrates V.), Stuttgart 1975.

When seated during singing, singers hold themselves erect so the respiratory tract can work properly and the space of resonance is maintained.

Figure 3. Our architectural base, the sit bones.

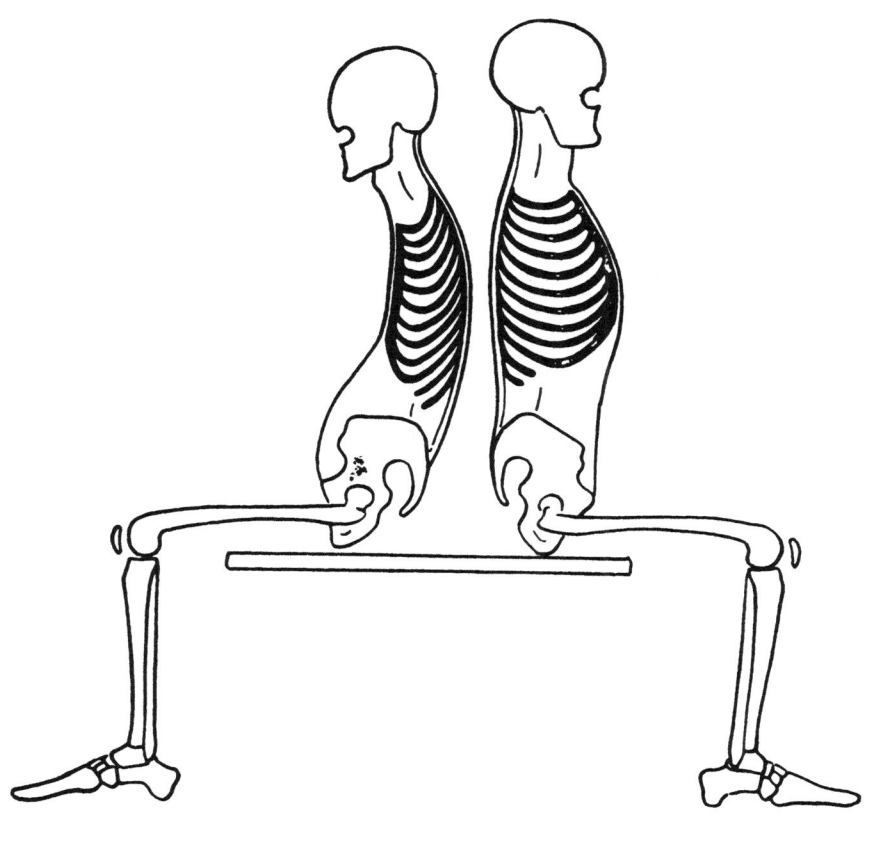

Incorrect alignment Correct alignment

Figure 3: Chas.V.W. Brooks, "Erleben durch die Sinne", (Sensory Awareness), S.84, Junfermann, Paderborn 1995.

Breathing

Unconscious breathing usually takes place nasally, whereas the quick inhalation during singing is a combination of oral and nasal breathing. To minimize the sound of breath intake and to have the placement of the next tone ready, the throat should be kept wide (like when yawning). Noisy breathing (as when inhaling forcibly) always indicates narrowness of the throat.

Singers should not inhale as much air as possible. Breath should "fall into the body" by itself. Therefore, the body needs to be wide. Movements that accompany the inhalation can help to activate the relaxed intercostals and flank muscles. This is a requisite for good breath control.

After vigorous exhalation, deep inhalation will follow automatically if the body is widened. That is why in all active respiratory movements when singing the exhalation of breath should be given priority. The famous *singer's support* (in Italian, *Appogio*) is nothing more than a deliberate regulation of the breath by slowing down exhalation.

Sound

Through their form, intensity of vibration, and degree of tension, the vocal cords determine height, loudness, and character of the sound. The vocal tract influences the vowels and the tonality. The anatomy of the pharynx produces the personal timbre of a voice. Efforts and tensions are often perceptible in the singers' faces. It is impossible to create a beautiful, free sound when the mind is distracted and negative.

Different emotions are transformed into sound by changing the shape of the vocal tract: Joy and astonishment widen the pharynx and let the voice sound round and soft. Fear, anger, and distrust narrow the throat, creating sounds that are hard, pressed, and shrill.

Placement

There are various **starting points** from which to achieve good placement of sound:
- The "third eye" (5) above the bridge of the nose is opened.
- The skullcap (4) can be imagined as the dome of a church.
- One can sing "into the mask" (3), the nose and bridge of the nose.
- One can feel the resonance in the breastbone (2).
- One can yawn at a note (1).

Figure 4. Additional starting points.

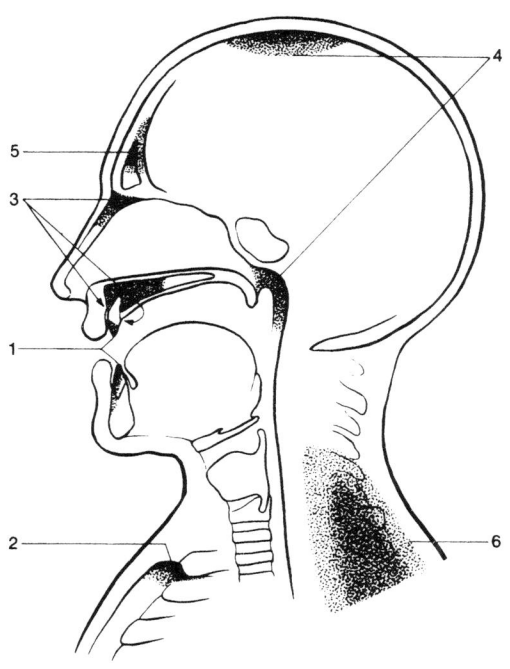

(1) incisors
(2) breastbone
(3) nose and bridge of the nose
(4) skullcap opening to the dome sound
(5) forehead
(6) neck

Figure 4: The starting points most commonly used by singers, from Husler/Rodd-Marling: Singen.

Imagery will encourage singers to unconsciously alter the spaces of resonance in ways that will help them place the tones. The placement image that will be most helpful depends on the vowel, the range, and the dynamic level. For instance, [i] in the middle range requires placement in front of the teeth (1) and at the third eye (5). In the upper range, [i] again accesses the front of the teeth (1) but requires more space in the sound. Finding the skullcap resonance is made easier if singers picture a halo over their head. This space is also necessary for the vowel [u], upper pitches, and soft singing.

Registers

The form of the vocal cords also influences the registers. In both female and male voices, there are three principle registers: head voice, middle voice, and chest voice.

Head voice:

Head voice is produced by vibrations of the edge of the vocal cords. It is the prevailing register of the high voices of women and children, and that of the soft sound of the complete range of the voice. The tones of the head register are soft, round, and comparable to those of a flute.

The vowels [u], ü [y], and closed [o] bring forth the head voice when sung *piano*. To maintain a healthy and beautiful voice, the head voice should work well in all registers and the vibration of the edge of the vocal cords should be present in loud tones as well.

Middle voice:

In the middle voice, approximately half of the muscle body of the vocal cords will vibrate depending on the height and loudness of the tone. At medium volume, the middle voice sounds clear and brilliant, and projects.

The vowels [e] and [i] start at the incisors and bring forth the middle voice.

Chest voice:

The chest voice (full vibration of the vocal cords) is used for full, strong intonation and the low registers. It is called forth by the vowels [ɑ] and open o [ɔ].

Without the vibration of the edges of the vocal cords used in the head voice, the chest voice sounds raucous and rough. Thus, the chest voice must be limited to the low register, the upper limit of which should be "d." A chest voice wound up too high is often heard from alto singers and from children who want to sing loud or are even asked to do so. It hinders the singers' ability to sing the high notes. They will sound too low, and there is danger of damaging the voice.

Male singers are sometimes able to sing in the spheres of female voices by using falsetto. In female voices, the highest registers are followed by the whistle tones. *Choral Vocal Technique* focuses on making the changes in register inaudible and giving the voice a homogenous character of sound (i.e., creating a balance between the registers). To achieve this, vowels and consonants are helpful in addition to the starting points discussed previously.

The vowel [u] gives support to the head voice and the dome sound. It opens the throat, vibrates at the same time as the breastbone and skullcap, and improves the tension of the lips. To produce a good [u], the lips must be wrapped around the vowel, and the tip of the tongue must touch the back of the front teeth.

The vowels [e] and [i] are formed with the tongue, the posterior part of which is lifted. They improve the brilliance in the middle register. With them as well as with ü [y], tenors can easily reach their high tones. Yet the high tones of female voices tend to sound hard when [e] and [i] are used and the lower jaw is kept fixed or held tight.

The closed [o] should contain a lot of [u] sound, with the lips wrapped around the vowel and a slightly more open mouth. For most singers, this is the easiest vowel.

The vowel a [ɑ] is the most difficult vowel. It is useful in two contrasting instances: It is helpful for women in the high register, or for a loud dynamic for both men and women; it also opens the chest voice. In loud singing, however, there is often danger of the tone sounding rough and raspy if it is too far back; it must be sung forward (as in the word "pasta") and not back (as in "father").

The consonants help to give the sound of the vowels the right resonance. The resonators "m," "n," "ng," "l," "v," "z," and flipped "r" aid the placement of the voice without straining it. The energetic pronunciation of "b," "p," "d," "t," "s," "ts," "sh," "ch," "j," "g," and "k" increases the mobility and flexibility of the tongue, lips, and lower jaw; activates the diaphragm; and is indispensable for understandable diction.

Exercises

Relaxation and Posture Exercises

For all exercises singers should have enough individual space to be able to move freely without hindering the singer on either side.

Exercise 1: Stand with your feet a shoulder's width apart. Feel your soles, imagining roots growing into the floor. Lean slightly into all directions (like a tree in the wind). Keep your feet on the floor and hold your spine erect. Gradually find the middle of your body and feel as if you are standing in the very center of a circle.

Exercise 2: Make circular movements with your feet, shaking them loosely. Make circular movements with your hands, stretching them in all directions; imagine it is autumn and the last apples (pears, plums) are to be gathered from the trees. Don't forget those that hang high up to the left and to the right.

Exercise 3: Imagine yourself suspended by a string (like a marionette). The string is attached at the highest point of your head at the back of the skullcap. If the string is loosened, your head lowers slightly, the lower jaw drops, and the eyes close. When the string is pulled up again, your mouth closes and your eyes open (look friendly!).

Exercise 4: Stand upright, arms hanging freely at your side. Slowly, one at a time, rotate your shoulders backwards: right shoulder four times, left shoulder four times, and then both shoulders together four times.

Exercise 5: Stand upright, arms hanging freely. Keep your head and neck up (as they were when you were a marionette), and look straight ahead. Now look over your right shoulder, stay like this for a moment, breathe out, and come back to your initial position. Look over your left shoulder, stay like this for a moment, breathe out, and come back to your initial position. When doing this exercise, your eyes should follow a horizontal line.

> NOTE: Every singer must decide for himself or herself how much stretching should be done. Imagine Pinocchio, with his long nose, looking about him curiously. The movements should be done slowly, and the shoulders should not participate in the rotation.

Exercise 6: The Royal Salute – Move your head slowly to the left and bow it gracefully (like a king or queen). Repeat the same movement to the right.

> NOTE: This exercise can be done in a sitting position as well. Rotating movements of the head should never be done with the head bent backwards!

Exercise 7: Hold your arms above your head, clasp your hands, and turn your palms out. Lift your hands up while breathing out. Do not bend backward, and be sure your knees remain slightly flexed. Breathe calmly, stretch upwards and feel your breath, which you should now clearly perceive in your lower back and abdomen. Release the tension gradually.

Exercise 8: Stand or sit upright. Lift your right hand above your head while bending your upper body to the left but not forward. Feel your breath in the right side. Come slowly back to your initial position. Repeat the exercise to the opposite side, lifting the left hand and bending to the right. Come slowly back to your initial position.

Exercise 9: Stand or sit upright. Let your head sink on your chest and roll forward, stretching vertebra by vertebra as your upper body sinks down. Move slowly, feeling each vertebra. Flex your knees slightly and let your arms hang heavily. Imagine a rolled-up leaf of a fern. Unroll very slowly, one vertebra at a time beginning with the lowest. Imagine the fern leaf slowly uncurling and reaching toward the sun. Leave your arms and head hanging loosely, and only at the end of the exercise lift the tip of your nose and open your eyes!

Exercise 10: To maintain a comfortable, upright sitting position, place yourself at the edge of the chair so the angle formed between your torso and your thighs is slightly larger than a right angle. Your feet may be shoulders' width apart, or you may sit with one foot placed under the chair with the weight on the ball of the foot and the heel raised. Feel your sit bones. Swing your upper body slightly to the right and to the left, forward and backward, until you are aligned and sitting correctly. Imagine two legs growing from your sit bones to the ground. Balanced on top is the upper body of the marionette (from Exercise 3).

Breathing Exercises

Respiration takes place passively. Singing does not require a lot of air, but its exhalation should be controlled.

When singers master the correct placement of the voice, they will discover they need less air for singing and, thus, will be able to sing longer phrases. They will give up the idea that with a lot of air one can sing particularly long passages. That is why the exhalation stands at the beginning of every breathing exercise.

Breathing exercises that deepen the breathing should not be repeated too often or done too long, as this might create problems for singers with a weak circulatory system. Breathing exercises should help the singers make use of the respiration that was so natural as a small child. The ribs swing out, the diaphragm lowers (which causes the abdominal walls to move out), and the pelvic floor lowers. Watching a baby, you see how the abdominal wall rises and falls with each breath. This is the natural breathing singers should adopt again. They should integrate this type of respiration as their normal breathing so it doesn't require conscious thought.

To avoid jeopardizing good alignment and good respiration, pay close attention to how singers sit down as they sigh. Remind them to sit in a good singing position. Proper alignment will aid the choir in observing their own breathing. Often the chairs available in rehearsal rooms, with their seats sloping back, are ergonomically unsatisfying; the use of wedge-shaped bolsters has proven helpful.

Exercise 11: Realize that respiration happens in three phases: exhalation–pause–inhalation. Exhale and prolong the pause until you feel a real hunger for air. At the moment of inhalation, let your lower jaw drop and relax your muscles. Exhale with a powerful blowing out of the air. During the next inhalation, which follows the pause, lift your arms as if embracing someone. Then exhale quickly and strongly on a "tsh" sound and let your arms come down.

Now exhale all of your air while imagining a dear friend coming through the door unexpectedly. Stretch your arms (which will cause the air to fall in) and exclaim with enthusiasm, "Oh, how nice to see you!"

Exercise 12: Repeat what you hear. (The director gives an energetic one-measure "sh," "psst," "ssst," or "ksst," or a one-measure pattern with these syllables.) During the following inhalation, let your jaw drop and your throat widen (as if yawning). This will ensure that the air flows in noiselessly.

> NOTE: This exercise activates the diaphragm; the abdominal wall is under tension. If the choir is familiar with this exercise, it is very useful in refocusing the choir's immediate attention whenever distracted.

Exercise 13: Blow the seeds off of a dandelion, or blow out a candle with a forcible "fff" or "tsh." After each exhalation, relax and let the air stream in.

Exercise 14: Exhale with a "tch." (You have just won the lottery!) Throw your arms up in surprise and elation as you let the air stream in through your nose and mouth at the same time. Keep your throat wide to diminish the breathing sound. Exhale with an "oy" sound.

Exercise 15: After breathing out, breathe in (as if smelling a beautiful flower or perfume). Now exhale slowly on "ssss" as you direct the flow of air to an exact point on the opposite wall. Keep the breastbone high and don't let it cave in.

> NOTE: Imagine the air from below rising upward along the inner side of the sternum.

Exercise 16: Sing a familiar song on "fff," "sss," or "sh." Since the impulses come from the abdominal wall, no additional sounds should be audible. Keep the vocal tract and the throat open, as when breathing in.

>NOTE: *Deck the Halls* and *My Bonnie Lies Over the Ocean* work well, in addition to a multitude of other possibilities.

Exercise 17: Sit on a chair like a tired coachman after a long, hot day driving tourists around in New York City's Central Park: bent forward, elbows resting on the knees, shoulders relaxed, and head hanging low. Be aware of your breathing, and deepen it with a few sighs.

>NOTE: This exercise is designed only to help singers feel the expansion in the back and to stretch the lower back. It in no way reflects good singing position!

Resonance and Relaxation Exercises

All of the exercises for resonance should be carried out in a low voice and in a velvety legato. Be sure the singers let the tones glide as though ascending on an escalator (rather than pushing them up a flight of stairs).

When singing on "m," the lips lie on each other lightly and the vocal tract is open in a yawning position. The singers should feel the vibrations at the sternum and the skullcap. The "m" should not be used in too high a register (not above a′), as it can easily narrow the throat.

When singing on "n" and "ng," the jaw should remain relaxed (no clenched teeth!). A Mona Lisa smile with raised cheekbones will help the sound ascend into the high range (no broad smiles). The singers should feel the vibrations at the incisors, the bridge of the nose, and the facial bones.

To reduce tension in the shoulder and neck area during the humming exercises, the singers may do the following:

- Move the head evenly and very slowly from one side to the other.
- Roll the right shoulder slowly, followed by the left shoulder.
- Put the elbows and hands on an imaginary water surface just below shoulder level and move them slowly to and fro without lifting up their shoulders!

The less self-conscious the singers are, the more noticeably the sound will amplify and make the room resonate. Rooms with sound absorbers (like carpets) and low ceilings are disadvantageous for such experiences.

Vocal Exercises 18–36

Exercise 18: Widen your body as though amazed, and listen inside.

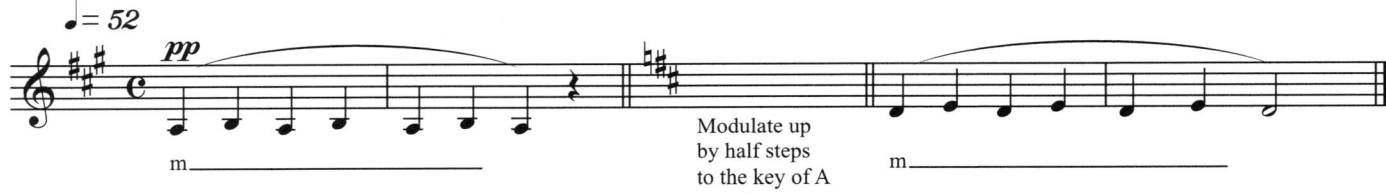

Exercise 19: Let your hands glide up softly, as if lifting a luxurious comforter.

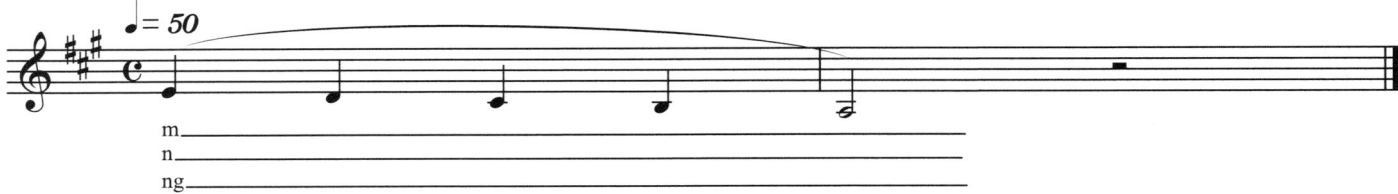

Exercise 20: Let the sound flow with pleasure; keep your breastbone up.

Exercise 21: Move your hands as though stroking velvet while singing. This exercise may be done as a round.

Exercise 22: Let your breath fall in without sound.

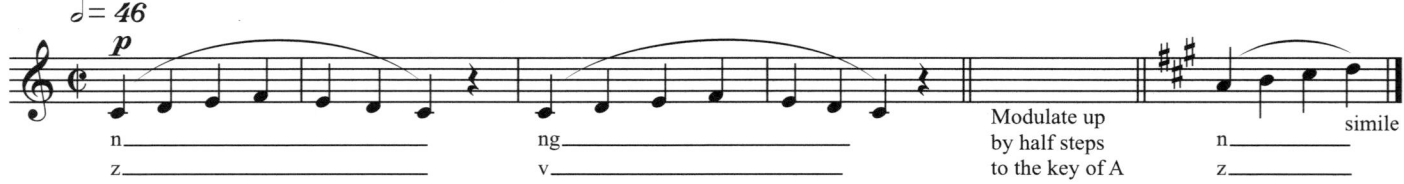

Exercise 23: Sing this as a very free round, with each singer singing at his or her own tempo. Before beginning again, take a measure to listen to the other singers. Imagine ringing a huge bell.

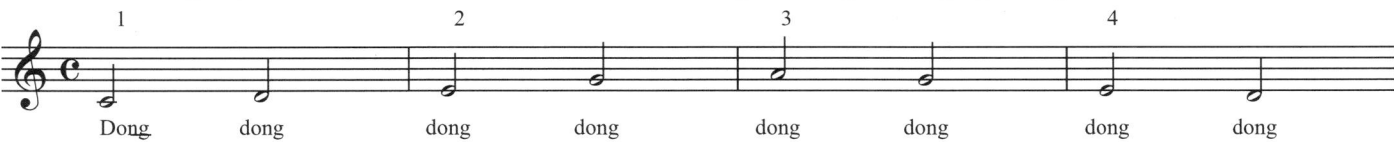

Exercise 24: Sing this as a round, using the given note values. Each singer should imagine singing in a huge rotunda, where the previous sound echoes downward as the new tone sounds upward. When adding dynamics, imagine that the round begins outside the cathedral, with the choir coming inside as the dynamic increases and then leaving the cathedral as the sound fades away.

Exercise 25: Don't interrupt the flow of the notes. Drop the lower jaw on each syllable. Let the resonators sound.

Exercise 26: Move through the vowel quickly. Use your arms to imitate a tennis player serving, or imagine yourself ringing steeple bells.

Exercise 27: Join the vowels closely; open the "third eye." Raise arms slowly while singing the descending notes.

Exercise 28: Sing in one forward-moving line. Don't mark time.

Noh nee noh nee noh nee noh nee noh nee noh nee noh
Doo vee doo vee doo vee doo vee doo vee doo vee doo
Noo mee noo mee noo mee noo mee noo mee noo mee noo

Modulate up
by half steps
to the key of G

Exercise 29: Relax and wobble the jaw on each note. Sing Italian vowels.

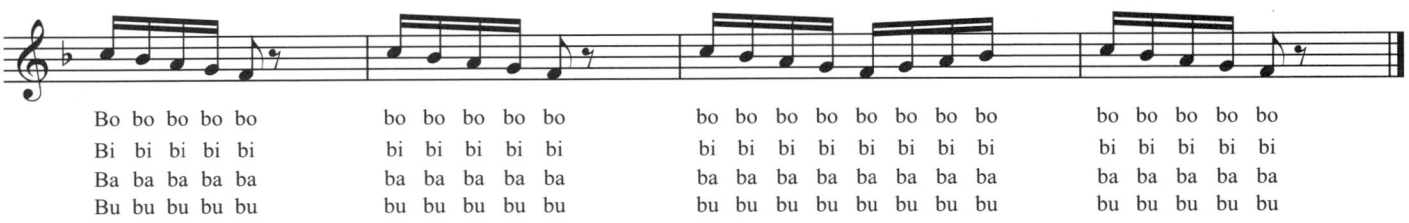

Bo bo bo bo bo   bo bo bo bo bo   bo bo bo bo bo bo bo   bo bo bo bo bo
Bi bi bi bi bi   bi bi bi bi bi   bi bi bi bi bi bi bi   bi bi bi bi bi
Ba ba ba ba ba   ba ba ba ba ba   ba ba ba ba ba ba ba   ba ba ba ba ba
Bu bu bu bu bu   bu bu bu bu bu   bu bu bu bu bu bu bu   bu bu bu bu bu

Exercise 30: Keep the jaw relaxed and flexible on each note.

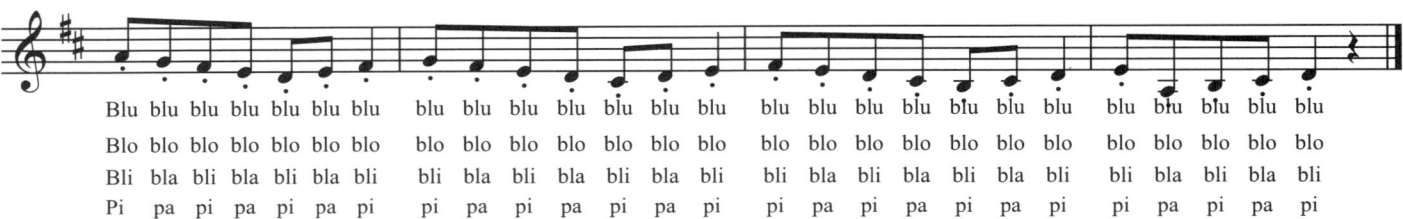

Blu blu blu blu blu blu blu   blu blu blu blu blu blu blu   blu blu blu blu blu blu blu   blu blu blu blu blu blu blu
Blo blo blo blo blo blo blo   blo blo blo blo blo blo blo   blo blo blo blo blo blo blo   blo blo blo blo blo blo blo
Bli bla bli bla bli bla bli   bli bla bli bla bli bla bli   bli bla bli bla bli bla bli   bli bla bli bla bli bla bli
Pi pa pi pa pi pa pi   pi pa pi pa pi pa pi   pi pa pi pa pi pa pi   pi pa pi pa pi pa pi

Exercise 31: Let the jaw drop freely as you move quickly through the consonants. If you do it properly, you will look like a ventriloquist's dummy.

Nu na nu na nu na nu na nu na
Ni na ni na ni na ni na ni na
Mi o mi o mi o mi o mi o
Zo ya zo ya zo ya zo ya zo ya
Tsim ba tsim ba tsim ba tsim ba tsim ba

Nu na nu na nu na nu na nu   na   Nu na nu na nu
Ni na ni na ni na ni na ni   na   Ni na ni na ni
Mi o mi o mi o mi o mi   o   Mi o mi o mi
Zo ya zo ya zo ya zo ya zo   ya   Zo ya zo ya zo
Tsim ba tsim ba tsim ba tsim ba tsim ba   Tsim ba tsim ba tsim

Exercise 32: Bounce an imaginary ball on the downbeat. Snap your fingers on the upbeats.

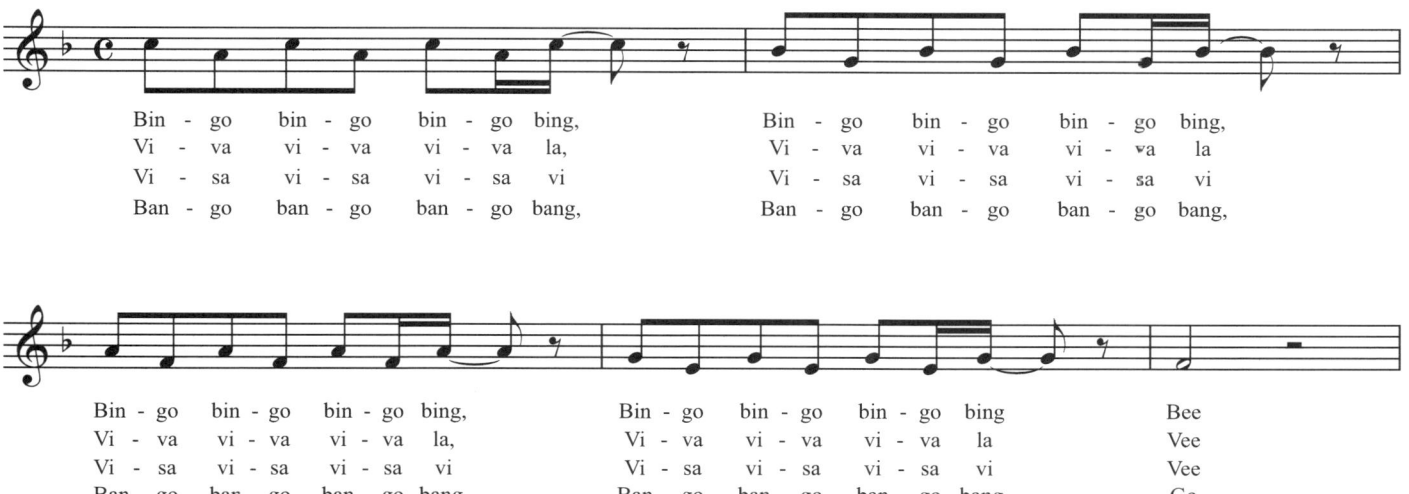

Exercise 33a: Pretend to turn a doorknob right and left as you sing. Repeat, modulating up or down by half steps.

Exercise 33b: This exercise can be done in minor, too. Continue motions and repeat, modulating up or down by half steps. Use German pronunciation for this exercise. The "s" should be pronounced [z] and the "e" on the second and fourth sixteenth notes of each beat should be treated as a schwa.

Exercise 34: Point on each note of the duplets and triplets as you sing.

Exercise 35: Relax the jaw, changing tongue position as necessary. When singing "bella," be sure to sing an Italian "l," with the tip of the tongue touching just behind the top teeth.

Exercise 36: Keep the jaw relaxed, changing tongue position as necessary. Sing to the end of the phrase.

Development of Sound, Equalization of Vowels and Registers Exercises

Apart from the resonators, the vowels are the carriers of sound. To make sure all vowels have the same quality of sound, rehearse the "vowel portamento" with the choir, which means the vowels vary seamlessly from one to the next. Thus, each vowel can profit from the neighboring vowel using the head voice character of [u], the brilliance of [e], the luminosity of [i], and the wideness of [a]. For evenness of vowel color, it is beneficial to sing with a "singer's pout," which is maintained also for [e] and [i]. It gives these vowels roundness and softness.

Vocal Exercises 37–52

Exercise 37: Open the "third eye" and let the vowels flow into one another closely. Keep the pout through all the vowels.

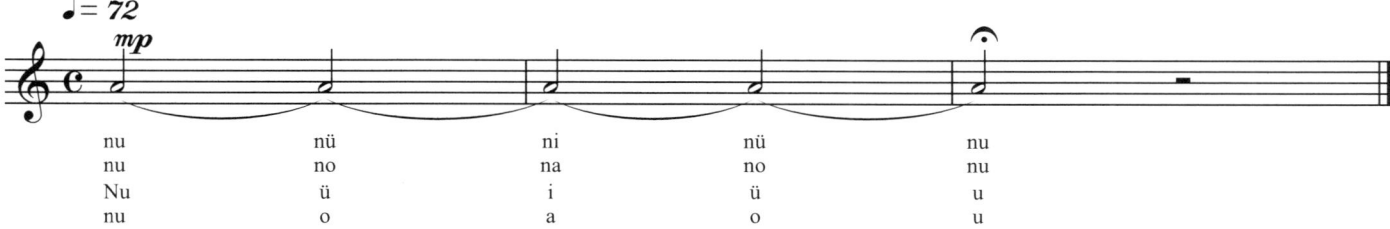

Exercise 38: Let the vowels flow into one another, raise your elbows, and trace a figure eight with your hands. (Sing as a round.)

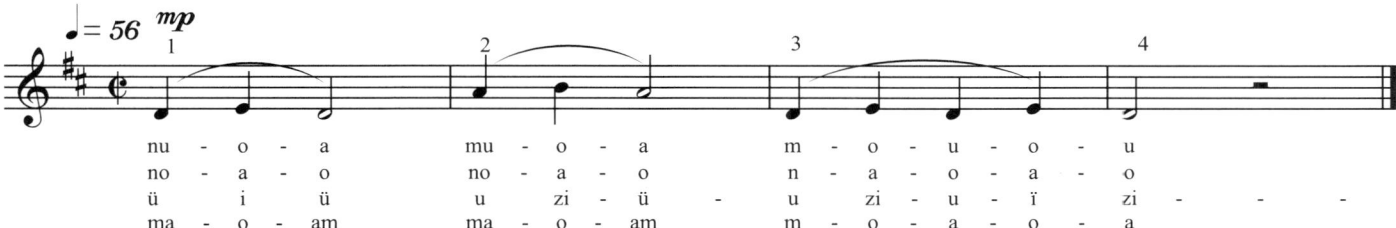

Exercise 39: Sing a joyous greeting.

Exercise 40: Let it flow. Sing pure vowels with no diphthongs.

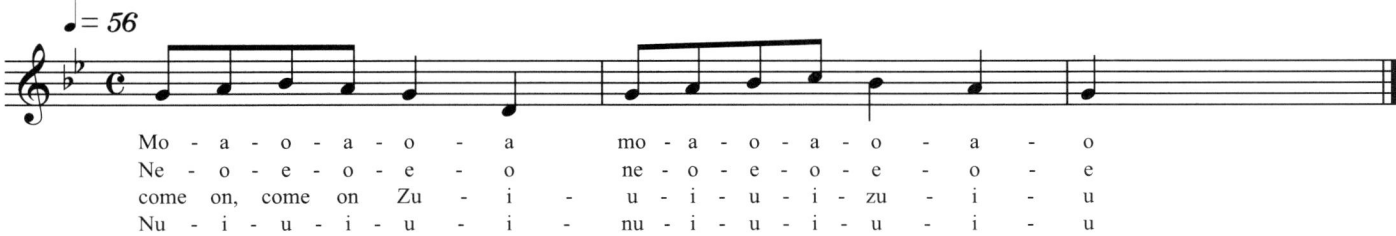

Exercise 41: Sing questioningly.

Exercise 42: Sing with enthusiasm while moving your hands upward from below (in the opposite direction of the scale).

Exercise 43: Sing while moving your hands in small circles (tune: Little Tommy Tinker).

Exercise 44: Draw a rainbow with your arms for each phrase while singing a smooth legato line. (This may also be sung as a round.)

Exercise 45: Let the sound flow (as in Smetana's *Moldau*). Use your arms to trace a figure eight while singing.

Exercise 46: Trace a large figure eight in front of you, beginning outward. (Sing as a round after the singers know it.)

Exercise 47: A minor little boat ride.

Exercise 48: Raise your arms, make soft and flowing motions to and fro with each measure; start outwards.

Exercise 49: The first part is like an impressionistic painting with all its little dots; use your hands to make the dots. The second part is smooth and legato. Use your hands as though making slow waves in the water. In the second system, sing the "ya" with a forward "a" as in pasta, rather than the "a" in father.

Exercise 50: Canon for adults and children, to be done with movement. Change movements for each line of the canon: (1) Wave to the right. (2) Wave to the left. (3) Shake hands to one side and remove an imaginary hat. (4) Shake hands to the other side and curtsy. (If this is sung as a Good-bye Canon, use the final lyrics, and have participants bow to the right, bow to the left, bow to the conductor, and wave good-bye to all.)

♩ = 112

1
Hal - le - lu - jah, Hal - le - lu - jah, Hal - le - lu - jah!
Gu - ten Mor - gen, Gu - ten Mor - gen, Gu - ten Mor - gen!
Good to see you, Good to see you, Good to see you!
Sa - yo - na - ra, Sa - yo - na - ra, Sa - yo - na - ra!

2
Hal - le - lu - jah, Hal - le - lu - jah, Hal - le - lu - jah!
Gu - ten Mor - gen, Gu - ten Mor - gen, Gu - ten Mor - gen!
Good to see you, Good to see you, Good to see you!
Sa - yo - na - ra, Sa - yo - na - ra, Sa - yo - na - ra!

3
Hal - le - lu - jah, Hal - le - lu - jah, Hal - le - lu - ia!
Gu - ten Mor - gen, Gu - ten Mor - gen, Gu - ten Mor - gen!
Good to see you, Good to see you, Good to see you!
Sa - yo - na - ra, Sa - yo - na - ra, Sa - yo - na - ra!

4
Hal - le - lu - jah, Hal - le - lu - jah, Hal - le - lu - jah!
Gu - ten Mor - gen, Gu - ten Mor - gen, Gu - ten Mor - gen!
Good to see you, Good to see you, Good to see you!
Sa - yo - na - ra, Sa - yo - na - ra, Sa - yo - na - ra!

Exercise 51: Minor canon for adults and children, to be done with different motions for each section of the canon: (1) Snap fingers on beats 2 and 4. (2) Spin hands quickly around each other as though winding yarn. (3) Spin in the opposite direction. (4) Throw arms upward on beats 1 and 3.

♩ = 120

1 Even eighth notes, not swing
Dum ba dum ba dum ba da

2
Da ba da ba da ba da ba da ba da ba

3
Da ba da ba da ba da ba da ba da ba

4
Doo wah doo wah doo ba da

Exercise 52:

Accompaniment for Exercise 52:

Marilyn Shenenberger

High Range Exercises

Above all, it is important to take away a singer's fear of the high range. Fearing that the tone "might not come," many singers try to reach the high range by using force, thereby obstructing the way all the more. Just like the lower notes, the high notes cannot be reached by using pressure.

On the contrary, it is much more helpful to imagine that the tones become slimmer and lighter towards the high range and that they float towards the skullcap and resound above one's head (imagine a halo). Keep the jaw relaxed, look pleasantly surprised, and open the "third eye" on the forehead.

To support diaphragmatic activity, it helps during range extension exercises to:

- Bend one's knees in a soft movement.
- Pull at an imaginary spring or rubberband.
- Pull down an emergency break on a train in front of one's body.
- Interlace one's hands in front of the chest and pull them apart.

Keep the upper body erect.

These dynamic exercises help to reduce tension in the area of the neck and shoulders. They have been described in ancient Italian schools, and Paul Lehmann in his lectures in the 1950s referred to these aids for vocal technique in singing lessons.

By concentrating on such dynamic exercises, it is easier to relax the vocal instrument. All exercises should take place with medium volume. The high notes should be imagined and sung a little more softly. Thus, the head voice of the female singers can sound well and will not be displaced by a wound-up middle voice.

In male voices, a wound-up chest voice must not push aside the middle voice. With sopranos, as well as with tenors, this strain on the voice can be heard as a stiffness of the tone. In soprano singers, it may also sound a little shrill.

Whereas soprano singers can manage the high range best with the vowel [a], tenors reach the high notes more easily with brighter vowels, such as [e] and [i].

The changing of registers is difficult for all voices. It may vary in each voice and become more or less obvious depending upon the vowel and volume. Exercises for vowels and for balance between the registers help to make those passages less audible.

Singing in an unaccustomed high range especially needs training. It is, therefore, advisable to go higher than the notes required by a piece during each group vocal technique session to activate the high resonances.

Care should be taken that these exercises do not last too long. The voices need to relax every now and again. This can easily be done with a sigh that starts at the top of the high registers and glides slowly to the deep range on [u], [o], or [a].

For ascending intervals that tend to be flat (e.g., an ascending fourth), it helps to imagine that the tone is not being pushed up a mountain from the bottom but rather is laying down on its top as if descending from above with a parachute. A movement of the hand from the back of the head upward and above the head to the front supports this image. Also, the idea of singing into one's own "dome" above one's head will give the high notes space.

Vocal Exercises 53–63

Exercise 53: Let the consonants resound.

Exercise 54: Throw a dart with each note you sing. Remember to relax the jaw on the high notes.

Exercise 55: Enunciate clearly. While singing, rhythmically mix a drink with both hands, using small energetic motions.

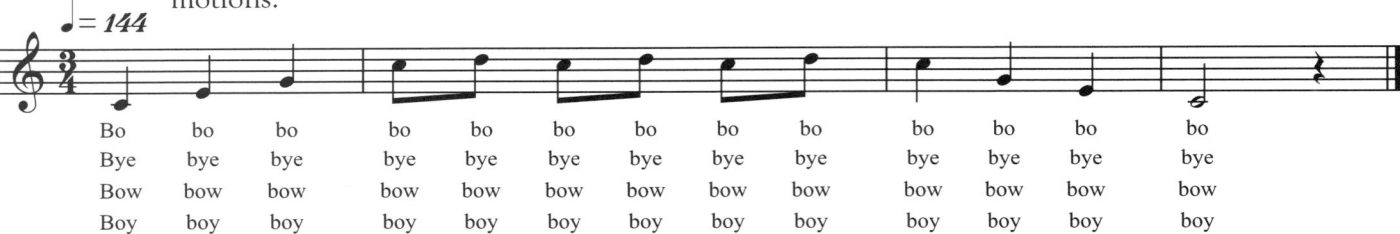

Exercise 56: Unlock your knees, then extend your hands downward and out as you ascend. Remember to keep the jaw free. Modulate up by half steps. (Lower voices may sing the optional part when the first part gets too high.)

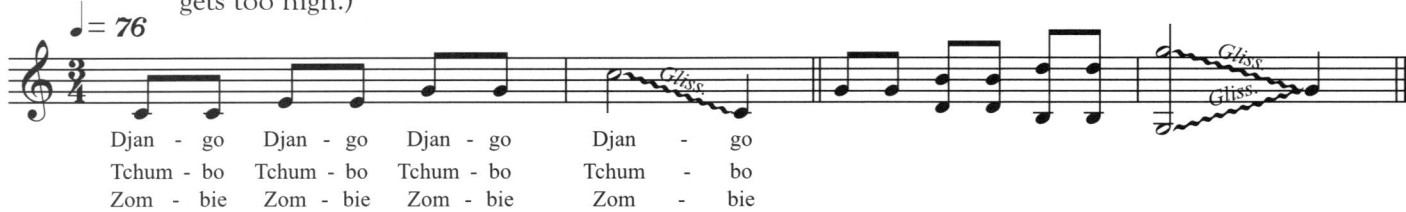

Exercise 57: Let the sound blossom on the high note, thereby maintaining the tension. Imagine you are smelling a fragrant flower.

Exercise 58: Continue singing on the vowel, singing the high note lightly. While singing, move your hands from behind the head at shoulder height, over the head, cascading down the front.

Exercise 59: Re-sing the vowel on each of the descending notes.

Exercise 60: In an admiring gesture of greeting, extend and open your arms with the high notes.

Exercise 61: Project the notes energetically, adding the hands to mime throwing each of the notes forward. Imagine the sound is situated between the eyes. (Lower voices may sing the optional part when the exercise goes higher.)

Exercise 62: Sing with energy, modulating up by half steps.

Accompaniment for Exercise 62:

Marilyn Shenenberger

Exercise 63a: Have singers walk while singing. Then add a fingersnap on beats 2 and 4 to the singing and walking.

Exercise 63b: As the exercise goes higher, alto and bass may sing the lower harmony.

Accompaniment for Exercise 63:   Marilyn Shenenberger

Low Range Exercises

The first rule for high range applies for the low range as well: There will be no vibration by applying force! Here, the image of Diogenes in his barrel would be helpful. Its acoustics are as good as those in a bathroom, and the tones will resound almost by themselves.

Once the singers have the feeling of wideness (expression of surprise or indignation), the voice can, in combination with bright vowels, gain more brilliance and intensity. Imagine singing through "rabbit's teeth." Moving the hand from bottom up helps to prevent the tones from becoming too deep. Another way is to imagine drilling the tone into the opposite wall like a laser beam; follow this beam of light with your hand.

Vocal Exercises 64–69

Exercise 64: Mime surprise. Embrace an imaginary barrel with your arms and sing into it. Lift the barrel a little.

Exercise 65: Sing as though surprised. Raise your hands, palms upward, as though carrying the tone. Higher voices should sing descant, as shown in measure 3, singing in the deeper register. In lyric options 2 and 3, "mai" and "vai" should be pronounced with a long "i" sound [a:I].

Exercise 66: Localize the French nasal sound in the nose. Use French pronunciations, and sing the vowel through the incisors. Remember, in French, the final "n" is not pronounced.

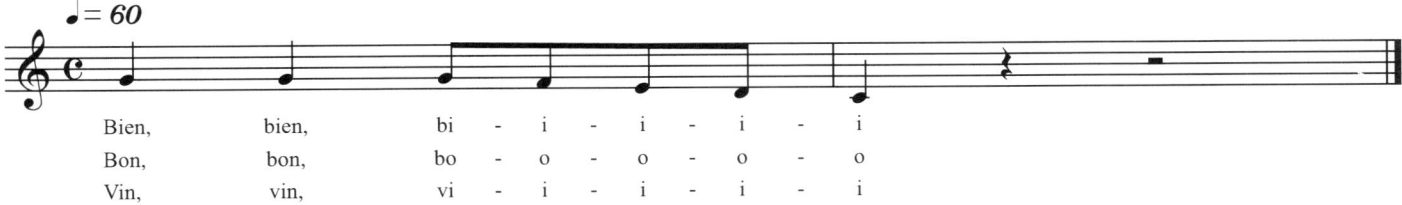

35

Exercise 67: Focus the sound toward the upper incisors, toward the "third eye" (in the middle of the forehead). Modulate down by half steps. In lyric 2, "tsio" is pronounced with a stopped "t" at the beginning, and in 3, "zia" is [zi-a].

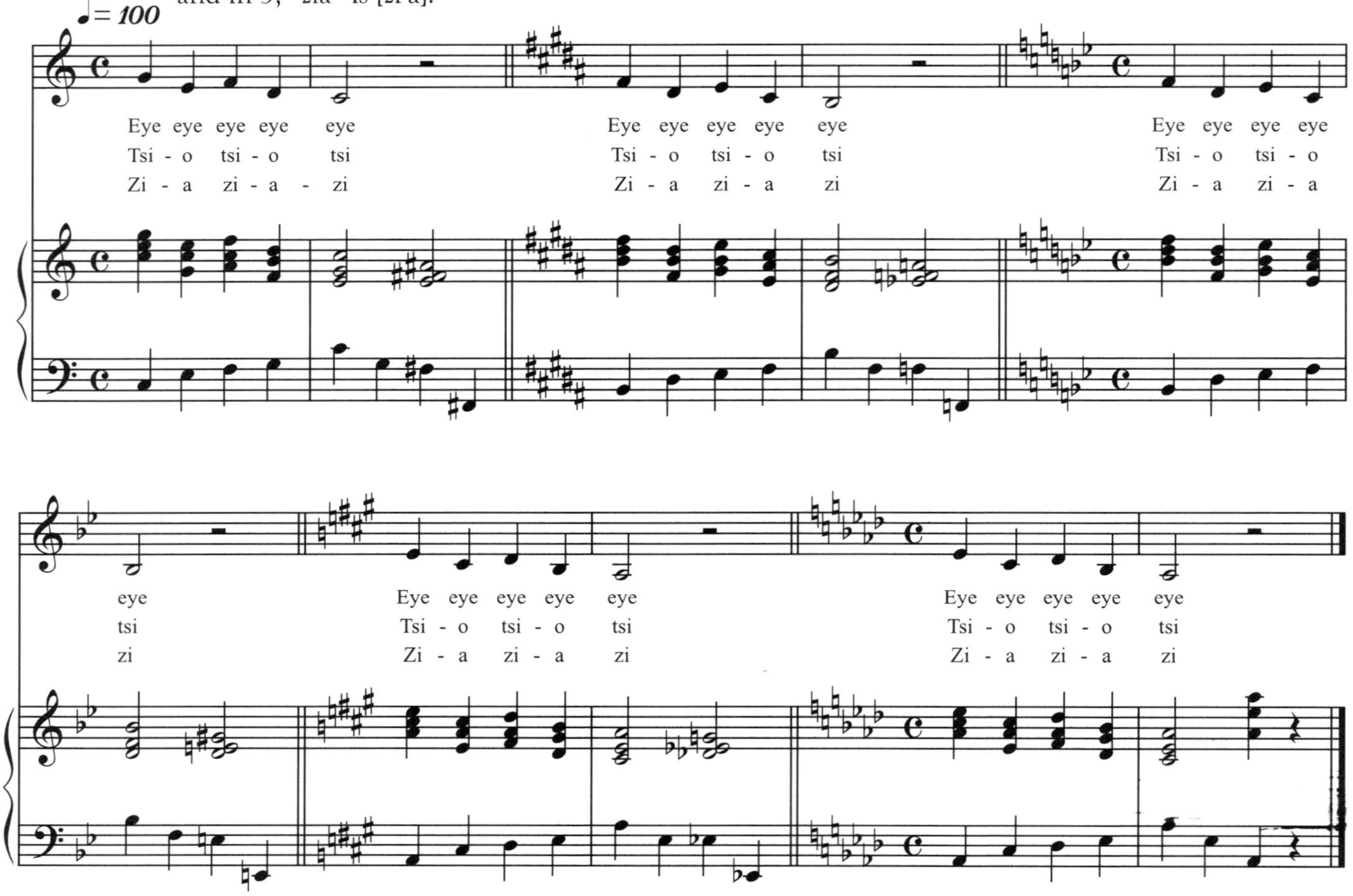
♩= 100
Eye eye eye eye eye
Tsi - o tsi - o tsi
Zi - a zi - a - zi
Eye eye eye eye eye
Tsi - o tsi - o tsi
Zi - a zi - a zi
Eye eye eye eye eye
Tsi - o tsi - o tsi
Zi - a zi - a zi
Eye eye eye eye eye
Tsi - o tsi - o tsi
Zi - a zi - a zi
Eye eye eye eye eye
Tsi - o tsi - o tsi
Zi - a zi - a zi

Exercise 68: Carry the deep tones, thinking of the "dome," raise the cheekbones, and smile with a puckered embouchure.

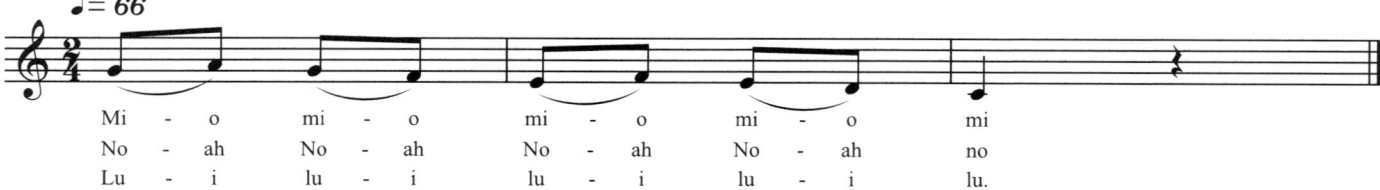

♩= 66
Mi - o mi - o mi - o mi - o mi
No - ah No - ah No - ah No - ah no
Lu - i lu - i lu - i lu - i lu.

Exercise 69: Sing with clear vowels. Sing into the "mask."

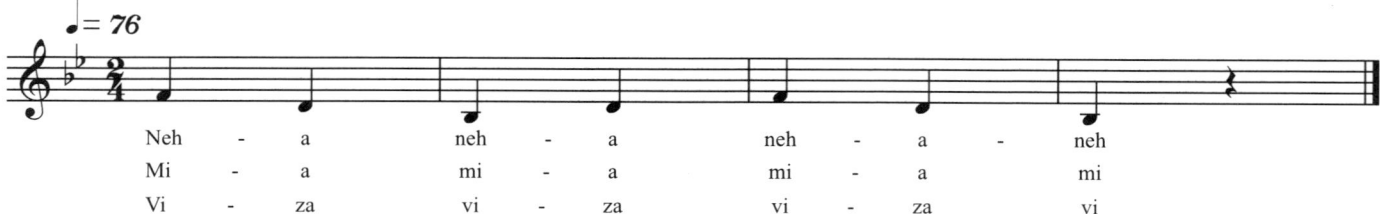

♩= 76
Neh - a neh - a neh - a - neh
Mi - a mi - a mi - a mi
Vi - za vi - za vi - za vi

Dynamics Exercises

It is a lot more difficult to sing *piano* than *forte* because the *piano* sound requires the same body tension as the *forte* sound. Unfortunately, many singers think that singing *piano* means singing with less energy. Therefore, *piano* passages often sound breathy and unsupported. To achieve a reliable *piano*, singers should imagine the tones being round and flute-like, emanating from a resonating chamber that is large and empty. This can be taught most easily with the consonant "c" in combination with [u], [y], or [o].

To let such a tone crescendo to *forte*, all that's required is to let it grow! The tone seems to start in the middle of the singer's head and then extend to all sides as it grows. The sound will grow without forcing the tone (and without causing the singer's face to redden), provided the singer pouts his or her lips gradually at the beginning of the crescendo while simultaneously relaxing the jaw.

Have the singers support the crescendo by adding hand movements. Have them put the fingers of each hand together in front of their forehead and pull their hands slowly down and outward. Or, ask them to reach out and up to grasp onto an imaginary rubberband that they pull toward themselves as they crescendo. "Put the sound round and bright into your head; then let it have legs growing down to the floor."

For a decrescendo, the tone takes the reverse path, as its "legs get shorter and shorter until the sound exists only in the heads of the singers." It will help if singers pretend to hold the rubberband taut, gradually allowing it to become smaller and smaller. This will help to avoid a release in the tension of the diaphragm, thereby avoiding an unsupported tone.

On notes that should have a light crescendo, let lovely smelling flowers grow that can be seen (and heard) for only a short time. The analogy of squeezing out a soft sponge may also work.

Vocal Exercises 70–76

Exercise 70: Imagine the sound starting in your head and extending to all sides as your head becomes bigger and bigger.

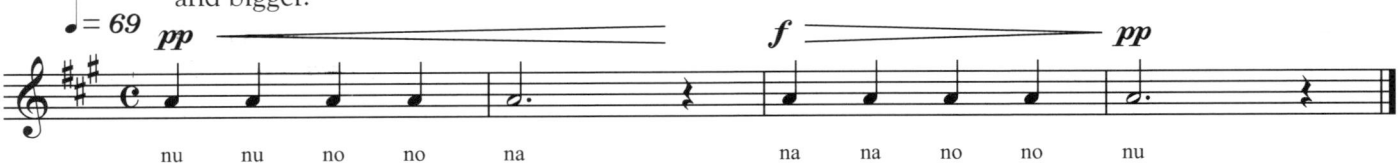

Exercise 71: Put your fingertips together in front of your forehead and pull them slowly outwards and down.

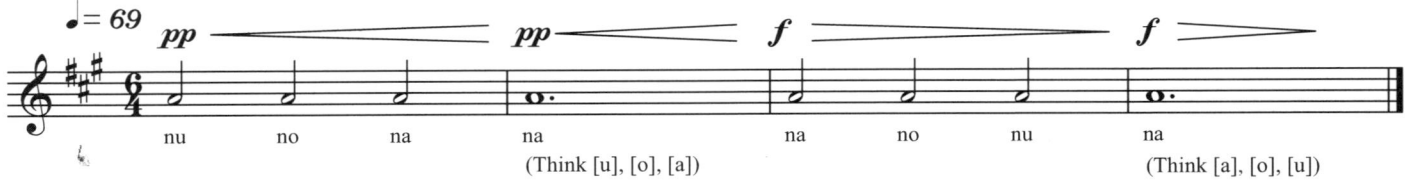

Exercise 72a: Lean your upper body forward and backward in quarter note rhythm.

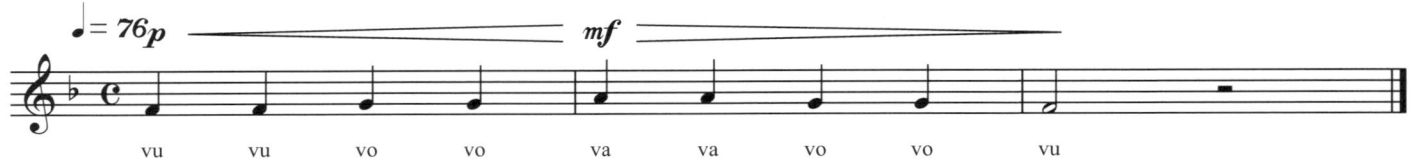

Exercise 72b:

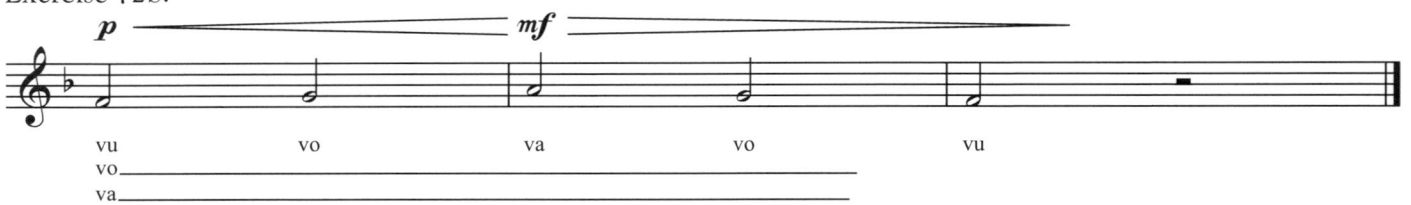

Exercise 73a:

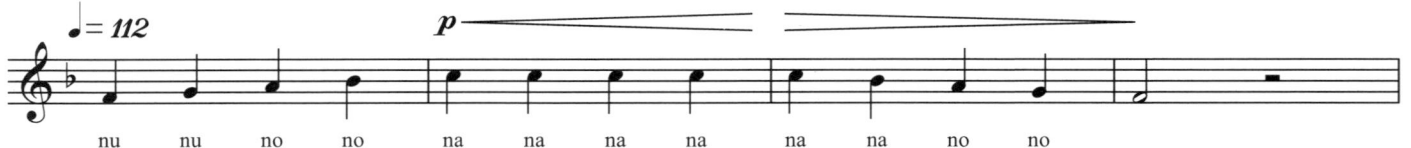

Exercise 73b: During the crescendo squeeze a lemon in each hand, and then gradually let go during the diminuendo.

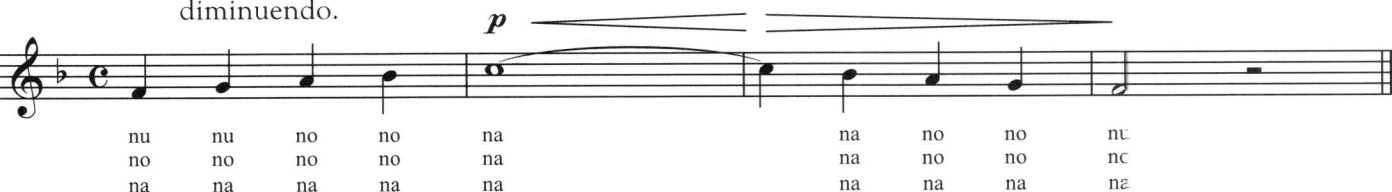

Exercise 74: Sing with admiration. Let the voice flow, think new vowels and, on the crescendo, squeeze out a sponge.

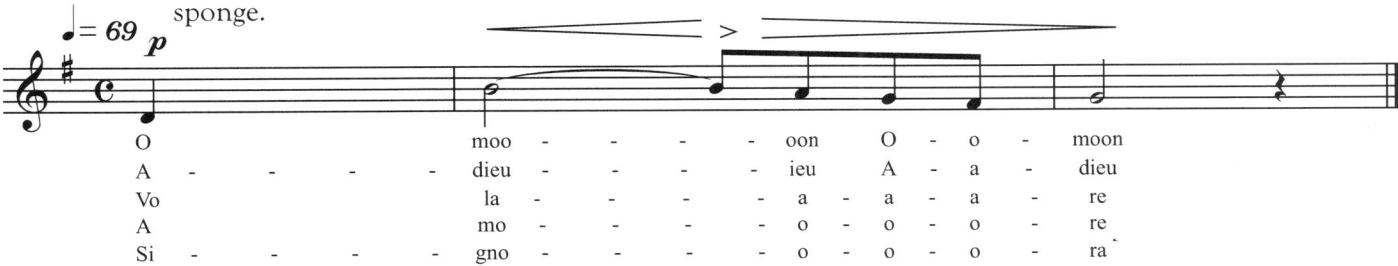

Exercise 75: Rethink the vowel on each note of the melisma.

Exercise 76: When singing softly, remember to enunciate clearly, think bright, and stay enthusiastic!

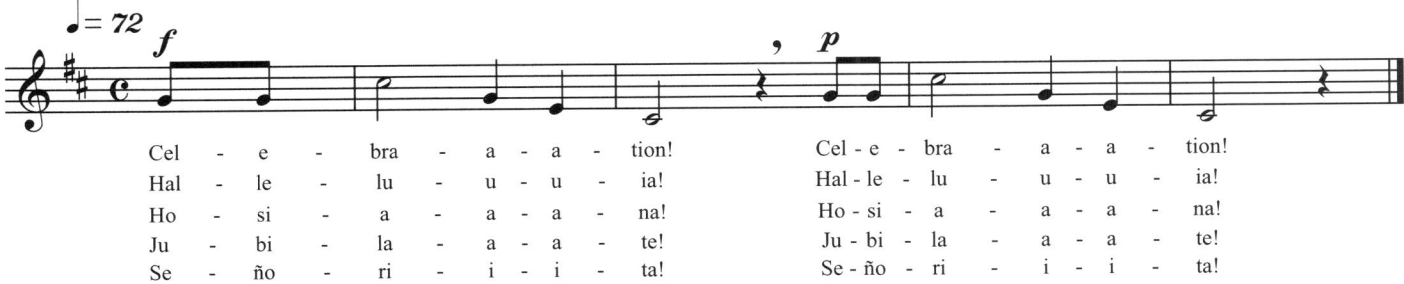

Diction Exercises

The beautiful sound produced through the vocal technique exercises will often be lost when singing on text, so it will also be necessary to practice the pronunciation of the text.

This includes exercises of relaxation, so-called gymnastics for the organ of speech. The stop-plosive consonants [b], [p], [d], [t], [g], [k] must not cut off the sound even though they interrupt the flow of air for a brief moment. Think of the sound and the consonants on two levels! The vowels build a soundtrack, which runs along evenly like a telephone line. The consonants sit on this line like birds. They can be heard very clearly but don't interrupt the sound.

Clear articulation and a relaxed tongue and jaw will, apart from the indispensable understanding of the text, also improve the placement of the voice.

The diphthongs, combinations of two pure vowels that are perceived as a single unit, are sung on the primary vowel; the second one is added only at the end of the tone. They are pronounced as follows:

[aɪ] = [a -ɪ] as in high, I, my

This sound is spelled in a variety of ways in German texts:

"ai", "ay", "ei", "ey" as in Mai, Bayrisch, dein.

[aʊ] = [a - ʊ] as in house, mouse, brown cow

This is the same sound as "au" in German texts, as in the words haus, baut.

[ɔɪ] = [o –ɪ] as in boy, foil, poise

This is the same sound as "eu" or "äu" in German texts,

as in getreu, Gebäude

In English and French, the y glide is an exception to the above rule. When singing [ju], glide past the primary sound of [j] quickly, and sing the second vowel longer.

[ju] = [j – u] as in Jubilate, cube, huge, use

When singing German texts, an "h" in the middle of a word (like in gehen, Mühe) is not pronounced, the first vowel is linked to the following one. In Spanish the initial "h" is not pronounced, and often the vowel that follows is linked to the previous word (as in "me hablo").

Italian diphthongs, unlike English and German diphthongs, require that the first vowel be longer and the second one shorter. If singing in Italian, consult an excellent diction book for a comprehensive list of diphthongs, glides, and triphthongs.

Vocal Exercises 77–87

Exercise 77: Keep the consonants energized. Pronounce [g] as a hard sound after the "ng."

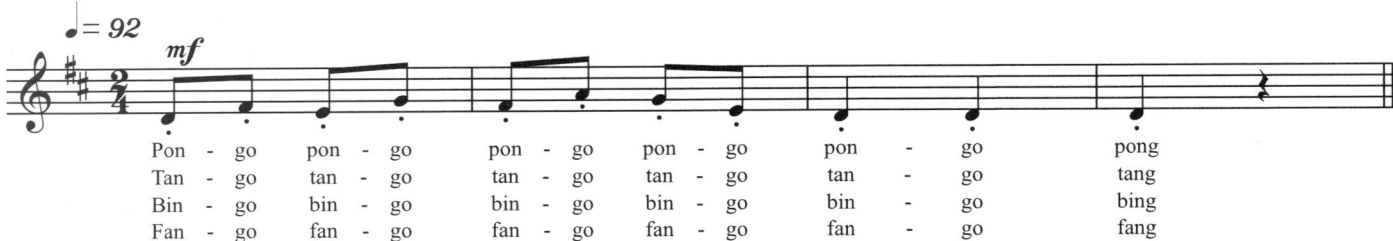

Exercise 78: Breathe in the vowel, keeping the jaw relaxed. Don't breathe during the pauses.

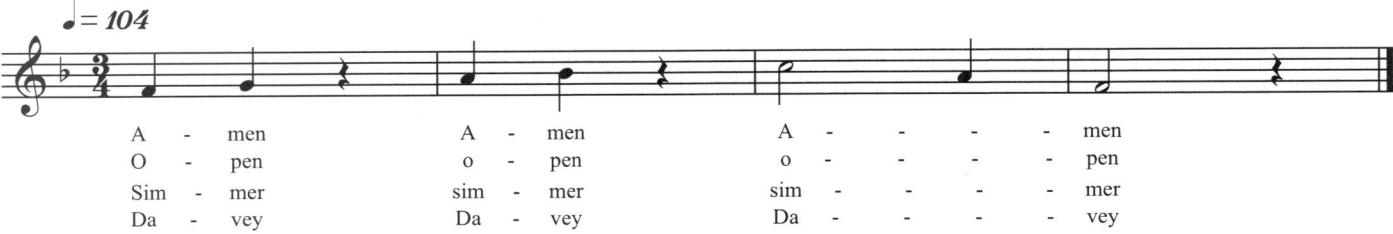

Exercise 79:

Exercise 80:

Exercise 81: Relax the jaw after each final consonant.

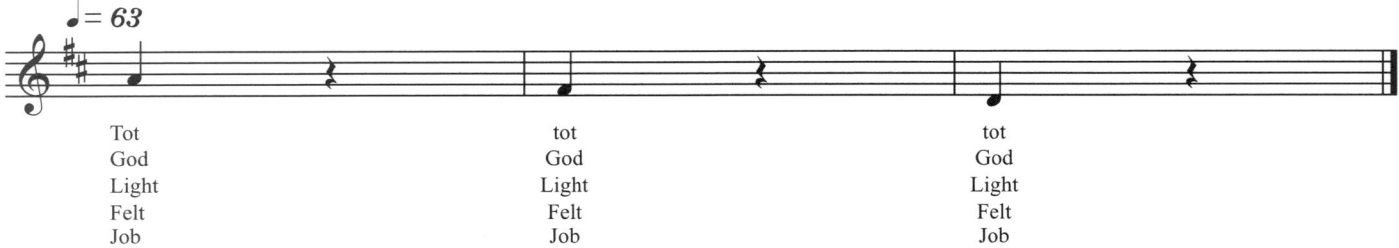

Exercise 82: In German diction, the "S" of "Singen" is pronounced as [z], and the "g" is not pronounced as a hard sound after the "ng." See page 40 for the correct diphthong pronunciation for lyric options 2 and 3. Remember that the "h" in "sehen" is silent. In the diminuendo of the second syllable, keep the sound the same, just softer.

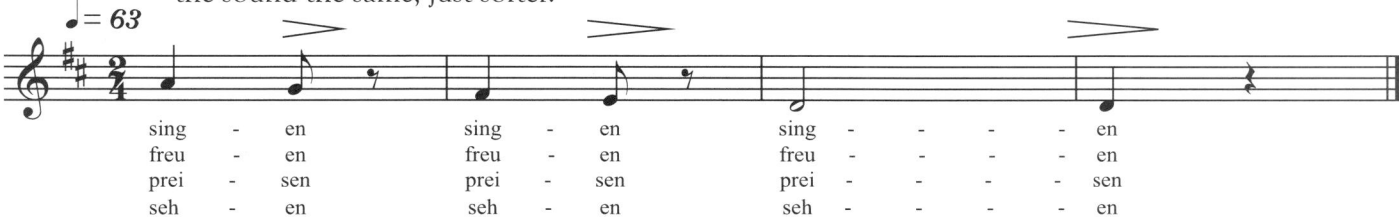

Exercise 83: Throw little arrows with each eighth note.

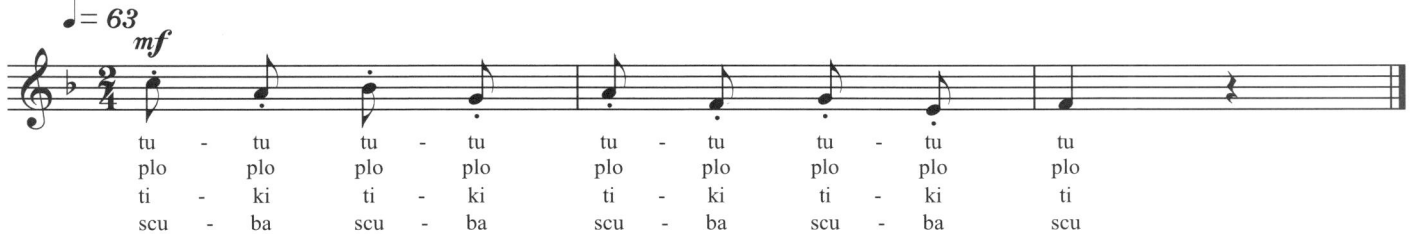

Exercise 84: Imagine a ball jumping on each quarter note pulse.

Exercise 85: Exclaim with enthusiasm. Round the lips into a "singer's pout."

Exercise 86:

Exercise 87: Good articulation is the essence of this exercise.

Legato, Staccato, Martellato Exercises

Legato can be practiced best with resonant sounds. Add to this an even, slow, but intensive movement of the hand while imagining a gently flowing river. The concentration on the movement while singing diverts singers from reverting to bad habits.

For the legato vocalises, imagine a new vowel on each note, gliding closely from one into the other. Make sure no "h" can be heard between the tones. Let the jaw drop very slightly on each tone.

For staccato, singers should make short, concise, and energetic movements of the hand. Using hard consonants will help to activate the diaphragm.

For martellato (e.g., coloratura passages in baroque music), a combination of staccato and legato is required: the even sound, the activity of the diaphragm on each note, and a relaxed jaw.

Vocal Exercises 88–94

Exercise 88: Link the vowels without putting an "h" between them. Sing lightly with flexibility and a sense of admiration. The first lyrics should be pronounced as letters of the English alphabet.

Exercise 89: To help achieve a soft connection between the tones, move your hands from the middle, down and out, and then back again.

Exercise 90: In the first measure, throw each tone with your hand while singing. In the second measure, stretch a taut spring between the hands.

Exercise 91a: Add quick movements of the hands, as though stirring a drink or beating an egg.

Exercise 91b: Think a new vowel on each note. Continue the movements of the hands and keep the jaw relaxed.

Exercise 92a: Move your hands as though mixing a drink while singing. Use the Italian vowel pronunciation for "do" [do] and "to" [to], rather than singing them like the English words "do" [du] and "to" [tu].

Exercise 92b: Keep mixing a drink and keep the jaw relaxed.

Exercise 93: In the first measure, pronounce the consonants energetically. In the second measure, think a new vowel on each note. Keep the jaw relaxed.

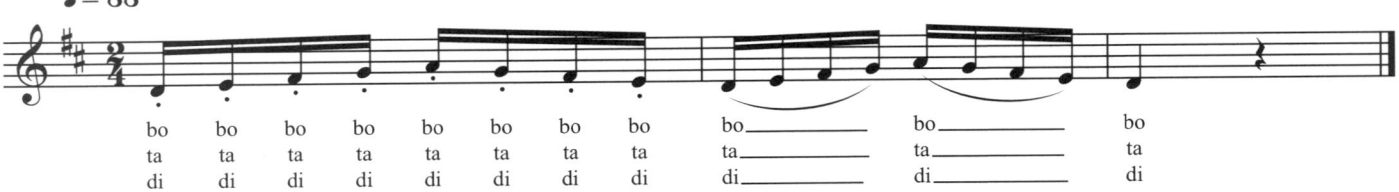

Exercise 94: For each note, think a new vowel. Keep the jaw relaxed.

Warm-up Exercises with Movement for Children

It is often helpful when doing vocal exercises with young children to surround them with a story. They will become actively engaged in the movement and in doing all the exercises without being self-conscious, and without realizing that they are doing warm-up exercises. The following story is one of the favorites of my children's choirs.

The Adventures of White Eagle

A little Indian boy was lying in his tent sleeping. The moon came up and shone on his face and woke him. He stretched and yawned, and remembered that this was the night he was to meet his friend so they could have a great adventure. So, he got up very quietly. [*Mime White Eagle's actions.*] He put on his pants and his shirt, and then he took the feather from the great white eagle that his father had given him the day before. He picked up his bow and arrow and tiptoed out of the tent. He stopped outside his tent to listen to see if anyone had heard him, and then sneaked cautiously away.

He walked over the hill until he came to a tall oak tree. He climbed up the tree and softly called out the secret signal to his friend.

Then he listened for his friend's answer. [*Mime listening with hand cupped to ear*] No answer.
He hooted a little louder . . .

. . . and then listened again.

This time he heard an echo.

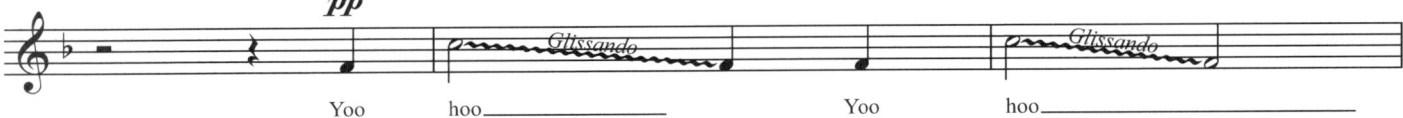

He did it one more time just to make sure. (*Repeat lines 2 and 3.*)

He climbed down the tree and started through the tall reeds, which made this sound as he pushed the reeds aside to walk through them. (*Mime action with hands while making the sound.*)

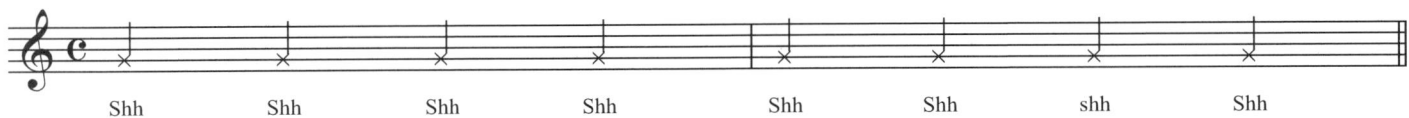

He jumped up to see if he could see his friend on the other side. (*Jump several times, as though trying to see over the tall grass.*) Then suddenly, he heard another sound. It was soft but getting louder.

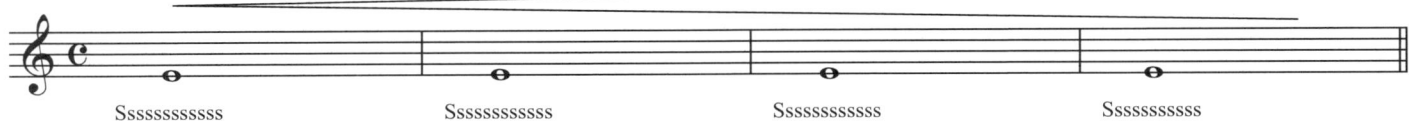

All snakes are afraid of loud noises, so he stamped his feet loudly.

The snake moved slowly away.

Then White Eagle set off through the tall grass again.

He came to the river, met his friend, and they sat on the bank to figure out what to do next. As they did, a bird on the other bank of the river seemed to be calling them.

Further down the bank they heard a woodpecker. (*If age appropriate, the two bird calls may be sung simultaneously by two groups.*)

A cloud covered the moon, and they suddenly became aware of all the other jungle sounds. They were very scared. (*Imitate jungle sounds as desired, depending on the age of the children.*) What do you do when you're afraid? SING!

The moon came from behind the clouds, and they called to their friends from the other village.

They could tell their friends from the other village were almost there.

They met their friends, and they all sang their Secret Song that tells how strong they are when they are together and how good it is to have friends. No adult had ever heard this song.

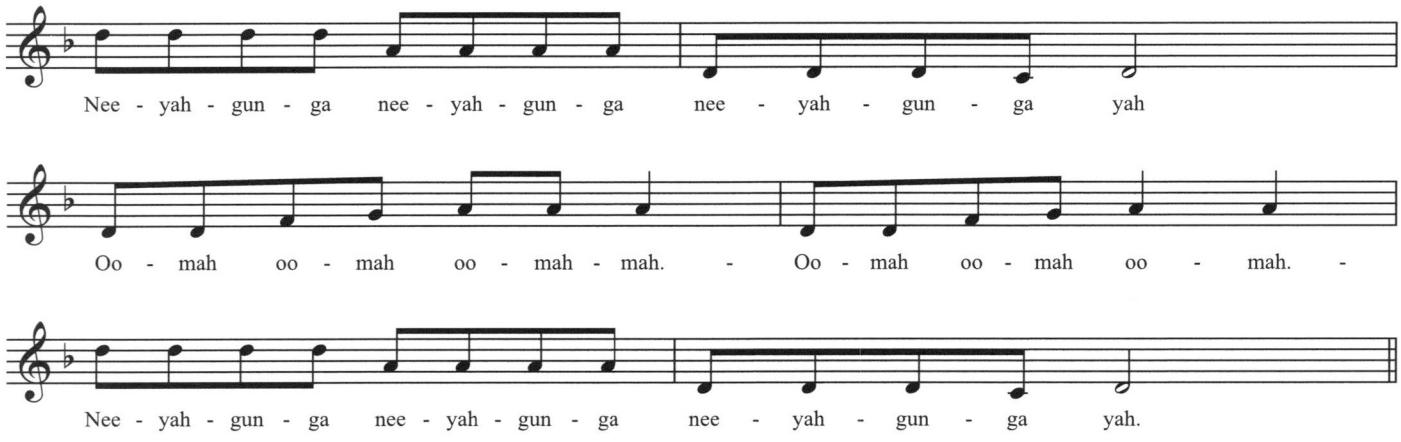

Dawn would be coming soon, and White Eagle had to get home quickly. It was his job to wake the village. He said good-bye to his friends and hurried back through the tall grass.

White Eagle went to each tent to wake up the village. First he went to the tent of Sweet Moon, who was a very beautiful Indian girl. He sang very beautifully to wake her. Then he went to the tent of the deaf Old Woman, and he had to sing very loudly to wake her. Next, he went to the tent of the grouchy man, where he sang very softly, and then ran away very, very quickly. Last, he went to the tent of Dancing Wolf, and so he danced and sang to wake Dancing Wolf. By then, the whole village was awake, and they all sang the beautiful song about the rising sun.

General Remarks

Depending on the duration of the rehearsal, the vocal technique exercises should take 15 to 20 minutes. Devote the first part to making the singers relax and prepare their body for these entirely other tasks.

In the second part, they will be prepared for the very requirements of the rehearsal. In the last part of the warm-up, work on long-term goals, such as the development of the high range, or martellato exercises.

The exercises should be as varied as possible and give the choir enough opportunity to relax. The best exercise in this respect is sighing! In an evening rehearsal, use more exercises to relax the body. Before singing in a religious service early in the morning, focus on exercises to wake up the singers.

In all cases, for adults, the first exercises on tones should begin in the lower register (female voices a-e´, male voices A-e´) at a *piano* volume and gain gradually in amplitude and intensity.

Choose simple exercises so the singers can learn them quickly and not have to think about the succession of the tones. Your singers will follow your example, so you must learn each new exercise thoroughly beforehand.

With all exercises, remember proper alignment and correct inhalation without loud breathing sounds. From time to time, let your singers breathe in on the vowels "o" and "u"; this will open their throats.

Choose exercises for group vocal technique from the different chapters (relaxation and posture, breathing, etc.) to match the needs of your choir. Mechanically sung exercises won't help at all. It is, therefore, beneficial to continually change exercises. However, when it is obvious your singers enjoy certain exercises, keep them for awhile.

Add exercises that relate to the technical demands of a piece to be rehearsed or a favorite exercise of the choir or a canon. At the end of the rehearsal, when required let everyone sigh on vowels.

Also while rehearsing, singers should be given aids for vocal technique or be offered an exercise to find the right placement of their voice in difficult passages. Don't practice too long in high registers, as this tires the voice.

Singers may need an occasional break, or they also may need to practice difficult passages a little slower until the succession of tones has become clear. In this case, exercise first in tone syllables and without text, enabling singers to concentrate on the melody first.

It is important for the success of all vocal technique exercises that the conductor be aware of the goal, keep listening (and watching!), and give aids for better execution. After awhile, singers will pay attention to their voice and its sound. In all the choirs I have worked with, most of the singers realized after only a short time that with the help of the exercises, many passages became easier to sing and sounded better. By and by, almost all singers will be ready to try out the unusual and new. Keep in mind, though, that just as in singing, it is not wise to force them.

The fact that during exercises singers are able to sing higher and sound better indicates that most singers become tense when confronted with high notes or multiple signatures. It often helps to sing these passages by heart.

And don't forget that especially in cases of difficulties, a smile can help as...

...SINGING GIVES JOY!

Israeli Canon and Taizé Canon

To show the choir how sound can be experienced through movement, let the singers walk about in the room while singing a well-known piece. Ask them to pay attention to the phrases and to the pulse of the piece by themselves. To try this out, I recommend the following canons.

Israeli Canon - Text is from Psalm 133:1 "look how nice and good it is that men should live together peacefully!"

Movement Sequence (by Tanja Kreiskott)

All singers take one step on each dotted quarter beat: 3 steps forward, then 1 step back. Divide the singers into 2 groups: an inner circle and an outer circle. One circle walks clockwise, while the other group walks counter-clockwise. Singers should have good alignment and look friendly at those who are walking toward them.

Taizé Canon - Do it in Unison first with hand movements, then as a round, and then in groups of three*.

Movement Sequence

The hands begin at the breastbone. During the first 2 phrases, they open very gradually up and out. During the third and fourth phrases, they slowly return to the starting position.
Divide the singers into groups of 3. The inside person leads the movement. The two outside people put their closes hand about two inches from the center person's hands, and mimic the movement of the center person.

Bibiography and Additional Resources

Brooks, Charles V. W. Erleben durch die Sinne. Jungfermannsche Verlagsbuchhandlung, Paderborn, 1979.

Brünner, Richard. Gesangstechnik. Feuchtinger und Gleichauf. Regensburg, 1984.

Ehmann, Wilhelm, and Frauke Haasemann. Handbuch der chorischen Stimmbildung. Bärenreiter, Kassel 1981.

Georgiades, Thrasybulos. Musik und Sprache. Springer, Berlin, 1954.

Göpfert, Bernd. Handbuch der Gesangskunst. Heinrichshofen, Wilhelmshafen, 1988.

Haasemann, Frauke, and James Jordan. *Group Vocal Technique*. Hinshaw Music Inc., Chapel Hill, NC, 1991.

Habermann Günther. Stimme und Sprache. Thieme, Stuttgart, 1978.

Haeflinger, Ernst. Die Singstimme. Hallwag, Bern, 1983.

Hofbauer, Kurt. *Praxis der chorischen Stimmbildung*. Schott, Mainz 1978.

Husler, Frederick, and Yvonne Rodd-Marling. Singen. Schott, Mainz, 1965.

Jordan, James. *The Choral Warm-Up*. GIA Publications, Chicago, IL, 2005.

Lohmann, Paul. Die sängerische Einstellung. Kahnt, Frankfurt, 1979.

———. Stimmfehler – Stimmberatung. Schott, 1966.

Martienssen, Franziska. Das bewußte Singen. Kahnt, Frankfurt, 1951.

———. Stimme und Gestaltung. Kahnt, Frankfurt, 1993.

Martiessen-Lohmann. Ausbildung der Gesangsstimme. Franzika Erdmann, Wiesbaden, 1957.

Parow, Dr. med. J. Stimmschulung. 2. überarb. Auflage, Paracelsus, Stuttgart, 1975.

Reid, Cornelius L. Funktionale Stimmentwicklung. Schott, Mainz, 1994.

Reusch, Fritz. Der kleine Hey /Die Kunst des Sprechens. Schott, Mainz, 1956.

Riesch, Anneliese. Lebendige Stimme. Stimmbildung für Sprache und Gesang. Schott, Mainz, 1972.

Rüdiger, Adolf. Stimmbildung im Schulchor. Handbuch für den Chorleiter. Chorheft. Helbling, Innsbruck, 1982.

Schwarz-Walter, Christa. Chorische Stimmbildung. Schultheiß, Tübingen, 1972.

Van der Vinne, Klaziene. In Koor: Natuurlijk zingen!, Broekmanns u. Van Poppel, Amsterdam, 1989.

Witte, Gerd. Grundriß einer chorischen Stimmbildung. Bärenreiter, Kassel, 1963.

About the Authors

SABINE HORSTMANN, instructor of Group Vocal Technique and voice at the Robert-Schumann Music University in Düsseldorf, has extensive experience working with singers of all ages. The focal point of her career is her intense work with a variety of choral groups, from children's choirs through adult choirs, and the further education of young conductors through her teaching of Group Vocal Technique and Conducting in Germany, Austria, Switzerland, and the United States. Horstmann studied voice at Folkwang Music University of Essen with Professor Jakob Stämpfli. She studied church music at Musikhochschule Köln, and in Herford with Professor Wilhelm Ehmann and Professor Frauke Haasemann, receiving the title Director of Church Music in 1986.

JAMES JORDAN is senior conductor at the renowned Westminster Choir College in Princeton, New Jersey. One of the most influential choral conductors and educators in America, his seventeen books covering rehearsal and teaching pedagogy, conducting technique, and the spirituality of musicing have had a dramatic impact upon teaching and conducting. At Westminster, he is conductor of the Westminster Schola Cantorum and the school's premier chamber ensemble, The Williamson Voices. This ensemble, which has premiered over thirty pieces in the past five years, has quickly become a voice for the composers of our time. The ensemble has won critical acclaim for its recordings of major choral literature. Dr. Jordan is also conductor of the professional choral ensemble, Anam Cara, heard on *Innisfree* and *Inscape*, recorded under the GIA ChoralWorks label.

MARILYN SHENENBERGER, collaborative accompanist and arranger, has been an integral part of James Jordan's cutting-edge work in the field of Choral Ensemble Intonation. She has written and recorded the *Accompanist Supplement* for *The Choral Warm-up Core Vocal Exercises* and *Learn to Listen*, a book designed to provide singers with a harmonic introduction to solfege. Shenenberger is co-author with Dr. Jordan of *Ear Training: Aural Immersion Exercises for Choirs*. She holds a Master of Music in Choral Conducting from Westminster Choir College and a Dalcroze Teaching Certificate from the Dalcroze School of Music in Manhattan. In addition to her accompanying work at Westminster Choir College, she is principal organist at Morrisville Presbyterian Church in Morrisville, Pennsylvania.